CATS OF THE Serengeti

by Carol Pugliano-Martin

Welcome to Serengeti National Park. This park is in Africa.

There are no swings in this park.
Wild animals live here.

Africa

Serengeti
National
Park

Lions, leopards, and cheetahs live in this park. They are wild cats.

leopard ▶

▲
lions

cheetahs ▶

Look! Do you see the lion? The lion has golden fur. Its fur is the same color as the grass. It blends into the grass.

Animals cannot see the lion coming.

▲
Hiding is important to lions. They can hunt without being seen.

This makes it easy for the lion
to hunt. It helps the lion survive.

Look up in the trees.
Do you see the leopard?

▲ Leopards climb in the trees and
look for food down below.

The leopard has golden fur with black spots. It blends into the trees. It is hard to see the leopard. This helps it survive.

Here comes a cheetah!
The cheetah has golden fur
with spots.

It blends into the tall grass.
This helps the cheetah survive.

The cheetah cub has long gray fur.
It blends into the shadows.
This helps the cub survive.

▲
A cheetah cub's fur also makes it
look bigger. This protects the cub.

The cats of the Serengeti
are great at blending in.
Blending in helps them survive!